Signs of

Winter

Signs of
Winter

Paul Humphrey

Photography by Chris Fairclough

W
FRANKLIN WATTS
LONDON • SYDNEY

This edition 2006

First published in Great Britain by
Franklin Watts
338 Euston Road
London NW1 3BH

Franklin Watts Australia
Hachette Children's Books
Level 17/207 Kent Street
Sydney NSW 2000

© 2001 Franklin Watts

ISBN-10: 0 7496 6958 6
ISBN-13: 978 0 7496 6958 4

Dewey Decimal Classification: 574.5
A CIP catalogue record for this book is available from the British Library

Printed in China

Planning and production by Discovery Books
Editors: Tamsin Osler, Kate Banham
Design: Ian Winton
Art Direction: Jason Anscomb

Photographs:
Bruce Coleman: 15 (John Cancalosi), 16 (Janos Jurka);
Corbis: 9 (Karen Huntt Mason); Linpac Environmental: 25;
Oxford Scientific Films: 24 (Anna Walsh); Photodisc 29 (PhotoLink);
Tony Stone Images: 20 (Timothy Shonnard), 22 (Phillip and Karen Smith)
All other photography by Chris Fairclough.

'When All the World is Full of Snow' from *Hurry, Hurry, Mary Dear!*
and Other Nonsense Poems © 1976 N.M. Bodecker.
Reproduced by permission of the publishers, J.M. Dent & Sons Ltd.

CONTENTS

Winter is here. Look for the signs of winter.

It is still dark when you wake up in the morning.

It's cold outside. Sometimes there is frost on the ground and on leaves and branches.

The windows on Mum's car are frosty, too.

When it's very cold, icicles form
and hang from the roof and gutters.

You have to wear a warm winter coat...

...and a scarf, hat and gloves.

You can see your own breath.

Your fingers and toes feel cold.

The branches on most trees are bare.

It is hard for the birds
to find food and
water.

Some birds feed on
winter berries.

You can put nuts and seeds in the bird feeder.

The farmer brings the cows into
the warm barn.

He ploughs the fields ready for planting in the spring.

Sometimes it is very wet in winter.

You have to spend more time indoors.

If you're lucky it snows, and you can build a snowman...

...or go sledging.

The snowplough clears the snow.

Salt and grit on the road melts
the snow and ice.

Winter evenings are dark and cold.
You turn on the central heating...

...or light a fire, and are happy to stay warm indoors.

What other signs of winter can you see?

When All the World Is Full of Snow

I never know
just where to go,
when all the world
is full of snow.

I do not want
to make a track,
not even
to the shed and back.

I only want
to watch and wait,
while snow moths settle
on the gate,

and swarming frost flakes
fill the trees
with billions
of albino bees.

I only want
myself to be
as silent as
a winter tree,

to hear the swirling
stillness grow,
when all the world
is full of snow.

N. M. Bodecker

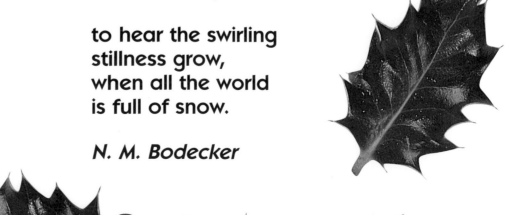

INDEX

It happened to me...
A new baby came home

Written by
Elizabeth O'Loughlin

Illustrated by
Ellie Dangerfield

First published in the UK in 2005
by PANGOLIN BOOKS
Unit 17, Piccadilly Mill, Lower Street,
Stroud, Gloucestershire, GL5 2HT.

Copyright © 2005 Bookwork Ltd.

A CIP catalogue record for this book is
available from the British Library.

ISBN 1-84493-021-1

Printed in the UK by Goodman Baylis Ltd.

GETTING HELP WHEN A NEW BABY COMES HOME

If you do not like having a new baby at home, it will help if you talk to someone about how you are feeling. You could talk to a friend, like the child in this book does, or to an adult that you trust. Or you can get help from ChildLine or the NSPCC. They will not tell anyone about your call unless you want them to or you are in danger.

Childline
(www.childline.org.uk)
If you have a problem, ring ChildLine on 0800 1111 at any time – day or night. Someone there will try to help you find ways to sort things out.

NSPCC
(www.nspcc.org.uk)
The NSPCC has a helpline on 0808 800 5000 which never closes. There is always someone there to talk to if you are unhappy, worried or scared about something in your life. You can also e-mail them on help@nspcc.org.uk

Not long ago, there were only
three of us – Me, Dad and Mum.
But now there are four of us.

The fourth one is called New Baby.
It has got another name, but I
can't remember what it is.

New Baby was in Mum's tummy. I don't understand how it got there. Dad says he put it there, but I still don't understand and it frightens me a little.

Now New Baby is in our home. I wonder why I am not enough for Mum and Dad. Why do they need somebody else as well?"

Everyone says that
I must love New
Baby. Sometimes I
do, and sometimes
I don't.

Sometimes I think it's the best new baby in the world, and sometimes I want to throw it in the dustbin.

"

"Mum often cuddles
New Baby very close.
It makes me feel funny
when I see them.
It makes me feel a
bit like I do when I'm
going to be sick.

Once, when I was watching them, Mum asked me if I was alright. I had to go, because I felt funny. But I said I was ok, and slammed the door. "

"My friend Julie has a new baby in her home too, so I talk to her about it.

Julie says that sometimes
she loves her new baby
and sometimes she
doesn't, just like me.

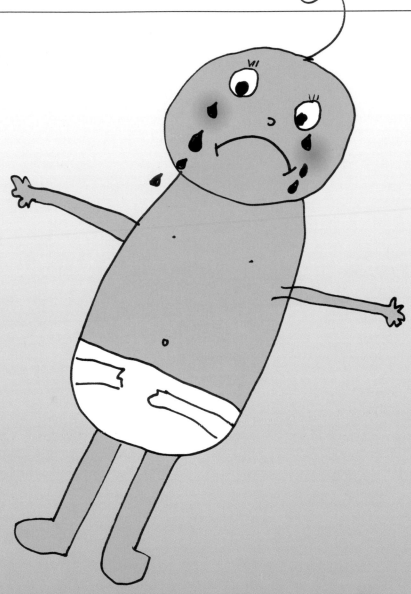

"I told Julie that New Baby doesn't even play with me. It just lies around all day and cries or sleeps.

Julie says I will get used to it soon. But I don't want to get used to it soon. I want New Baby to go away so I can be the only one again. "

How can I love New Baby when Mum spends all her time with it? She used to spend all her time with me.

And she has changed since
New Baby came. She walks
very slowly and speaks very
quietly. And when I want
her to play with me, she
says she is too tired. „

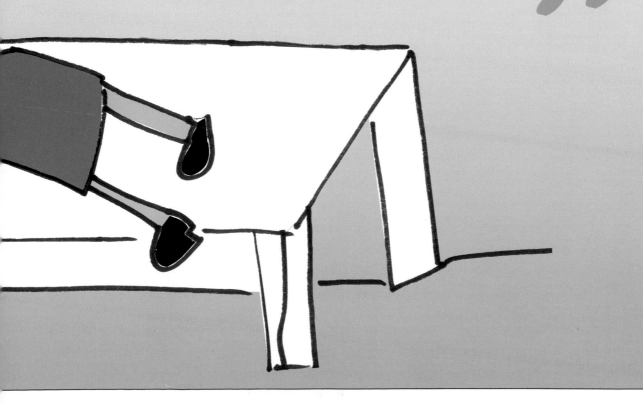

"I want to be New Baby. Then Mum will spend all her time with me again. So I cry and climb on Mum's knee. And I try to be just like New Baby.

Sometimes Mum lets me cuddle up to her, and then I feel a bit better. But often she doesn't let me cuddle up. She says I am too big.

I told Dad it's unfair that Mum is always with New Baby when she used to be always with me. Dad said that Mum was never always with me, because she was with him as well.

I think Mum loves New Baby more than me. Dad says she doesn't, but I don't believe him. I wonder what I can do to make Mum love me best again. „

Sometimes I laugh and shout and run very fast so that Mum will look at me and not look at New Baby.

But she tells me to be quiet because New Baby has gone to sleep. She doesn't understand that I want to be New Baby so she won't need two of us any more.

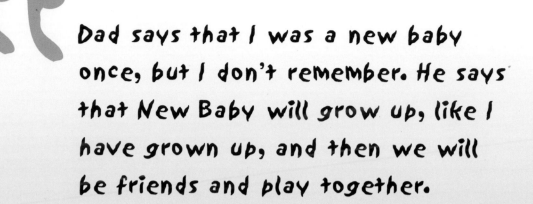

Dad says that I was a new baby once, but I don't remember. He says that New Baby will grow up, like I have grown up, and then we will be friends and play together.

I hope we will be friends, but I'm not sure. Perhaps we will be friends, but not all the time.

"My friend Julie says that she
likes having a new baby at home,
because now she isn't the smallest.

And she can tell the new baby what to do, like her mum and dad tell her what to do. "

"Julie says it's good to have a new baby at home, because her mum can't watch her and the new baby at the same time. Now she can do some things that her mum doesn't know about. Perhaps my New Baby isn't so bad after all!"

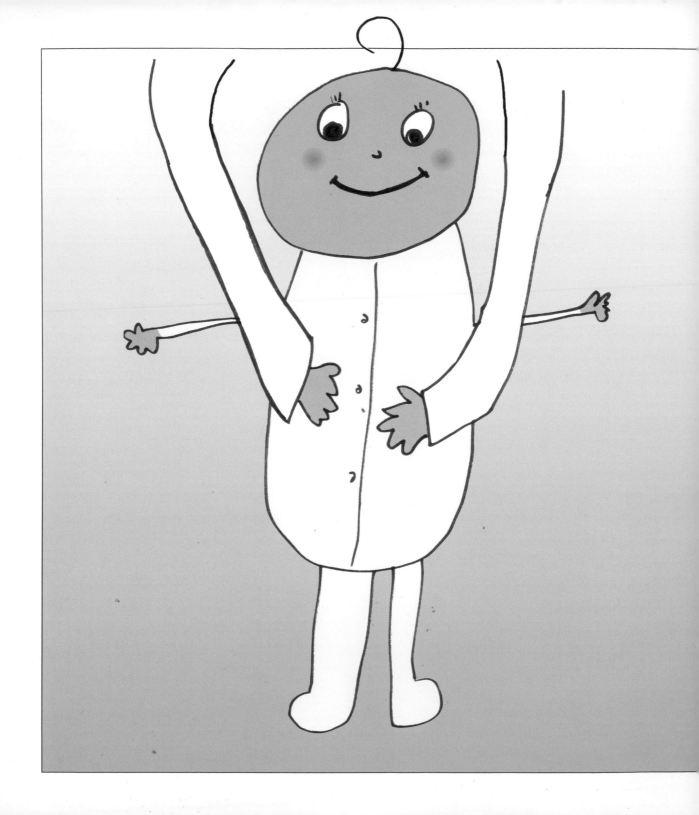

"Today, Mum let me hold New Baby on my lap. He felt all soft and warm, and smelt nice. I liked the way he cuddled into me. And I felt big and strong, like a big bear I saw in my book."

"I've just remembered that
New Baby's name is Dan.
I'll tell Julie tomorrow."